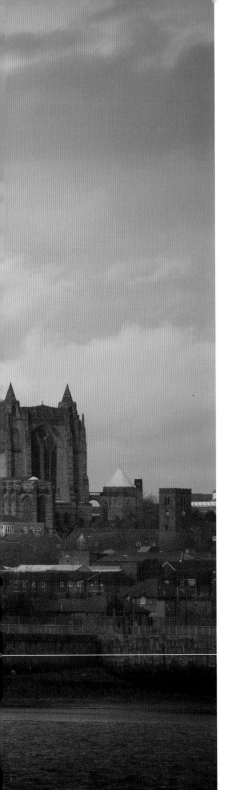

The poet called L 'one of the the world'. city skyline and the river Mersey and is visible for many miles around.

Its construction over a 74 year period (despite two World Wars and the depressions of the 1930s and 1970s), is an extraordinary achievement which speaks volumes for the spirit of local people, for their vision and determination.

This guide offers an introduction to the building, which became the life's work of its architect, Sir Giles Gilbert Scott. But the Cathedral is not just a magnificent piece of architecture. It is the lively mother church of its diocese, dedicated to the Risen Christ. It is a place filled with people day by day, who gather to attend exhibitions and performances, to eat and drink, to worship and pray, and to learn more of what it means to be a follower of Christ in the 21st century.

Liverpool Cathedral dominates the surrounding landscape just as the cathedrals in Durham and Ely do. How can something so massive be so recent?

The story of Liverpool goes back over 800 years to 1207, when a small settlement on the banks of the Mersey was granted a royal charter. It was only in the 1700s that Liverpool's significance as a port began to grow, with the import of cotton, sugar, and tobacco from America and the West Indies.

Though the city cannot be entirely proud of this increased prosperity (since much of it was based on the slave trade), many

Photo © Paul McMullin

of the buildings which grace Liverpool today were built on the wealth and confidence of this 'golden age'.

The Diocese of Liverpool was formed in 1880, but it would be a further two decades before a Parliamentary Bill received royal assent in 1902, authorising the purchase of St James' Mount as the site for the building of the new cathedral.

Photo © Liverpool Cathedral

'We must give to God not that which costs us nothing, but the very best that Liverpool can afford.'
Bishop James Chavasse

The Cathedral from the River Mersey, an iconic part of the Liverpool skyline. Most of the buildings on the riverfront date from the 20th century.

5

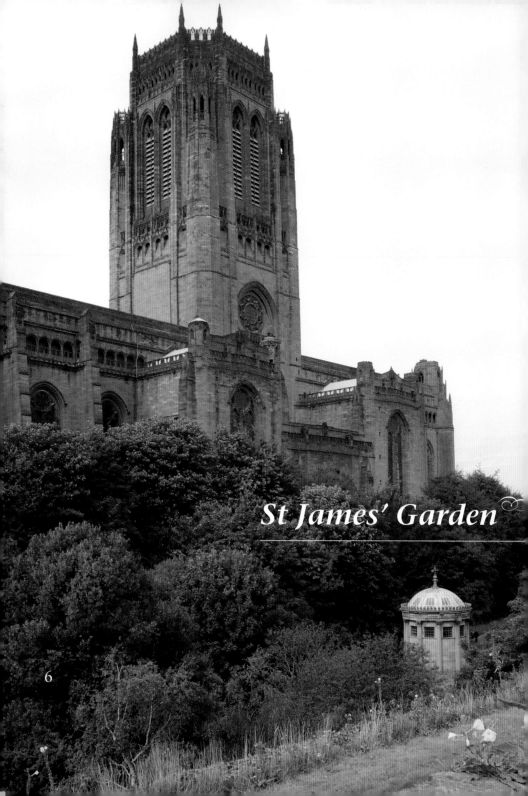

St James' Garden

J ust to the east of the Cathedral lies a hidden treasure: St James' Garden. During the 18th century, this was a quarry providing much of the stone for the building of Georgian Liverpool. In the 19th century, when the quarry could no longer supply quality stone, it was developed as a cemetery by the architect John Foster Junior. The Parthenon-like building at the entrance (now known as the Oratory) served as the mortuary chapel.

By the time the cemetery was closed in 1936, almost 60,000 people had been buried there, including Kitty Wilkinson, the social reformer, and William Huskisson, the statesman and local MP.

At the heart of the park is the Chalybeate (a mineral water) spring.

The domed structure is the Huskisson monument. William Huskisson became the world's first recorded rail casualty when he was run over by Stephenson's Rocket.

Liverpool Cathedral is the largest Anglican Cathedral ever built, and a position under the vast central tower is the best place to appreciate the skill of the architect in creating a truly breathtaking Great Space. The pointed arches lead the eye heavenwards, an effect achieved by the inventors of this early English 'gothic' style in the 13th century and adopted again by Victorian architects.

The architect of Liverpool Cathedral, Sir Giles Gilbert Scott, was able to take medieval practices to new extremes by using 20th century materials and techniques. The result is a structure that generates a feeling of awe in most visitors through the use of light, space, and height.

Scott (a Roman Catholic) was only 22 years old when, in 1902, he won the design competition to build the Cathedral, never previously having designed so much as a small chapel. The design evolved considerably over the course of the next six decades in which Scott worked on the building.

8

The Dulverton Bridge is one of the most unusual architectural features in the Cathedral. Visitors who use the audio tour finish the tour by climbing it and are rewarded with a panoramic view whilst hearing the organ and choir.

The Great Space

9

The Bells

The bells of Liverpool Cathedral are the highest and heaviest peal in the world. They were funded through a generous bequest for the purpose, left by Thomas Bartlett.

The 13 swinging bells weigh 17 tonnes (16.5 tons). At the centre of the peal stands Great George, (15 tonnes, 14.5 tons), which is too heavy to be swung and so hangs in one position and is struck with a hammer. Great George is bigger than Big Ben and second only in size to Great Paul of St Paul's Cathedral in London.

It took ten hours to haul Great George by rope into the bell chamber through an opening in the central vault of the Great Space.

Photo © Liverpool Cathedral

11

The stained glass over the Great West Doors is the design of the artist Carl Edwards (who worked on many of the windows of the Cathedral between 1948 and 1978), together with the architect Frederick Thomas (who had succeeded Scott upon the latter's death in 1960).

This *Benedicite* window takes its inspiration from an ancient text calling on all creation to sing praise to its Creator: 'O all ye works of the Lord, bless ye the Lord'.

The window covers 1600 square feet (149 sq m) and contains six tons of glass (200,000 pieces) plus nine tons of the special bronze bars that hold it secure. It was completed only shortly before the service of thanksgiving and dedication in October 1978, which marked the completion of the building and was attended by Her Majesty Queen Elizabeth II.

Below the window, the pink neon art installation 'For You' is the work of Tracey Emin, rendered in her own handwriting.

At the top of the Benedicite window at Liverpool Cathedral is a figure of Jesus, reflecting the dedication of the building 'to the Risen Christ'.

Benedicite Window

14   *The massive statue of the Risen Christ over the West Doors outside the Cathedral was the last work by the sculptor Elisabeth Frink. It was erected just a few days before her death in 1993.*

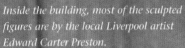
Inside the building, most of the sculpted figures are by the local Liverpool artist Edward Carter Preston.

The Good Samaritan *by Adrian Wiszniewski. The Good Samaritan – strikingly portrayed as a woman – holds out a cup of water.*

Art and the Cathedral

For centuries, churches and cathedrals have provided the inspiration and springboard, as well as the financial resources, to encourage some of the Western world's greatest music and visual art. Liverpool Cathedral is no exception. It houses works by (among others) five Royal Academicians: Craigie Aitchison, Tracey Emin, Christopher Le Brun, Adrian Wiszniewski, and Elisabeth Frink.

15

Sir Giles Gilbert Scott

A portrait of Sir Giles Gilbert Scott by Reginald Grenville Eves in 1935. It is from the RIBA Library Drawings and Archive Collections.

16 *A scale model version of Scott's original design for the Cathedral (with two great west towers) is on display in the Derby Transept.*

The architect of Liverpool Cathedral, Sir Giles Gilbert Scott, came from of an architectural dynasty, which included his grandfather (Sir George Gilbert Scott), his father (George Gilbert Scott Jnr), his uncle (John Oldrid Scott) and his brother (Adrian Gilbert Scott).

At the age of 19, Giles was indentured to Temple Moore, one of the leading practices of the day. Three years later, he won the design competition for the building which was to become his life's work. Scott was knighted the day after the consecration of the Cathedral in July 1924.

Among his other famous buildings are the University Library in Cambridge, Battersea Power Station in south London and Bankside Power Station on the Thames (now converted into the Tate Modern). He was also responsible for the design of the classic red telephone box.

Scott died in 1960 and was buried just beyond the entrance steps of the Cathedral. The building was completed 18 years later.

There is a memorial to Sir Giles Gilbert Scott directly under the central tower, in the middle of the Great Space. (The function rooms downstairs are also dedicated to him).

17

Music plays a vital role in the life and worship of the Cathedral. The choir consists of about 70 men, boys and girls. The seven choral services sung throughout the week in term-time are inspirational, and the stunning skill of the singers is enhanced by the remarkable acoustics of the enormous building.

The grand organ, by Henry Willis III, is the largest pipe organ in Britain and one of the largest cathedral pipe organs in the world, with 10,268 pipes, ranging from the enormous ten-metre (32-ft) pedal stops to the tiny two-centimetre (3/4 in) Spitzflote. There are two consoles – the organist can either play from the conventional position in the organ loft or use the mobile console on the floor of the cathedral for recitals and concerts.

A mobile console is also available to support worship at the west end of the Cathedral.

The Lady Chapel is served with its own instrument.

The Organs

18

The Grand Organ's famous Tuba Magna (on 50" pressure) is one of the loudest organ stops in the world – almost equivalent in decibels to a jumbo jet on take-off!

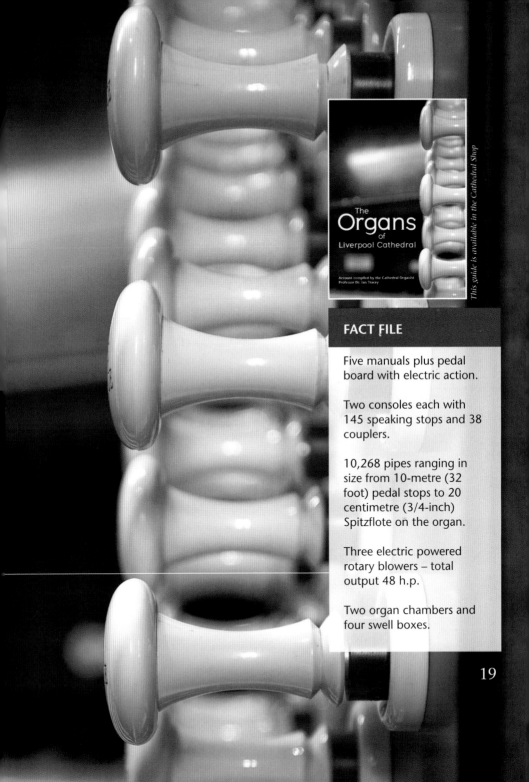

The
Organs
of
Liverpool Cathedral

Account compiled by the Cathedral Organist
Professor Dr. Ian Tracey

FACT FILE

Five manuals plus pedal board with electric action.

Two consoles each with 145 speaking stops and 38 couplers.

10,268 pipes ranging in size from 10-metre (32 foot) pedal stops to 20 centimetre (3/4-inch) Spitzflote on the organ.

Three electric powered rotary blowers – total output 48 h.p.

Two organ chambers and four swell boxes.

The High Altar

The central act of worship in the Christian Church (usually called 'Holy Communion', or 'The Eucharist', meaning 'The Thanksgiving') recalls the Last Supper Jesus shared with his disciples, when he gave them bread and wine as symbols of his body and blood sacrificed for them.

The Last Supper is illustrated in the lower panel of the reredos, the decorated screen behind the High Altar, richly carved from sandstone and embellished with gold leaf. The Crucifixion is shown in the other central panel with further scenes of Christ's Passion to each side. The outer panels show the Nativity and Resurrection.

The *Te Deum* window rises above the reredos, with the figure of the Risen Christ at its highest point. The *Te Deum* is an ancient hymn of praise, beginning 'We praise thee, O God, we acknowledge thee to be the Lord...'. The hymn celebrates the acclamation of God's majesty by the whole church.

The High Altar itself is made of panelled oak, and the top is a single piece of wood.

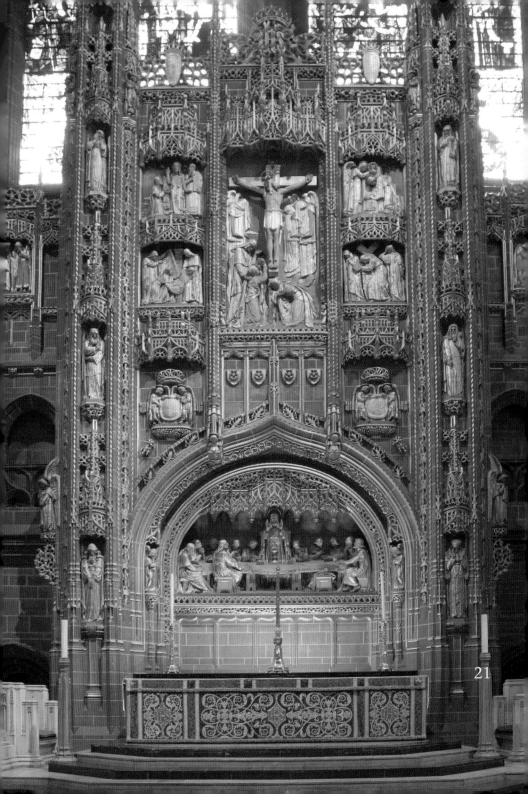

21

The extravagant style of the Lady Chapel may reflect the influence of G.F. Bodley, a prominent architect who (until his sudden death in 1907) assisted the inexperienced Scott.

The Lady Chapel, completed in 1910, is used on occasions when a more intimate form of worship is needed, such as weddings or funerals.

All the original stained glass in the Lady Chapel was destroyed in 1940. The restored windows, re-using the original theme, celebrate the role of women in the history of the Church.

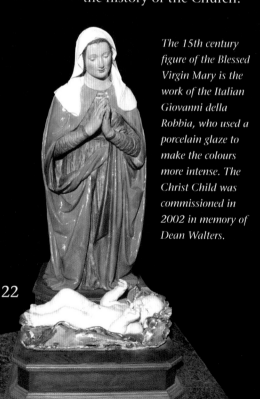

The 15th century figure of the Blessed Virgin Mary is the work of the Italian Giovanni della Robbia, who used a porcelain glaze to make the colours more intense. The Christ Child was commissioned in 2002 in memory of Dean Walters.

22

The Lady Chapel

23

Noble Women Windows

The role of the women in the history of the Church is further celebrated in other stained glass windows. At the west end of the Lady Chapel and on the staircase are the 'Noble Women' windows featuring portraits of women famous for their heroism.

Among them are Julian of Norwich, the medieval mystic; Christina Rossetti, the poet;

and Elizabeth Fry, the prison reformer. Some (such as Kitty Wilkinson, Josephine Butler and Catherine Gladstone) have a strong Liverpool connection.

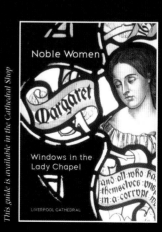

This guide is available in the Cathedral Shop

24

The Liverpool Girls Friendly Society, founded in 1875 and run by women for women had almost 200,000 members at its peak.

and all

Butler

champions

of purity

1828

1906

gift of associates members
Girls Friendly Society
of Liverpool

The Nostrils

For almost one hundred years, members of the Cathedral Choir have climbed the steps through 'the Nostrils' before every act of choral worship.

LIVERPOOL CATHEDRAL

AWESOME
AND
INTIMATE

A SPIRITUAL JOURNEY FOR YOU

This guide is available in the Cathedral Shop

'Awesome and Intimate' – an intimate space with a view of the awesome.

Behind the High Altar is the narrow corridor known as 'the Ambulatory'. It is here that the Cathedral choir assembles before and after each act of choral worship, and is led in prayers of dedication and dismissal.

The choir processes in two lines, passing through each of the stepped passages into the Sanctuary, under the two arches at either end of the Ambulatory. These arches are, perhaps predictably, known as 'the nostrils'. They offer an unusual perspective on the Cathedral, looking west. The pleasing way in which the nostrils frame the Great West Window makes this particular view a favourite with photographers.

In the windows high on the west wall are figures of representative English, Scottish, Welsh and Irish saints. High above the steps at either end of the Ambulatory are curious balconies, connected to passages above the Quire Aisles.

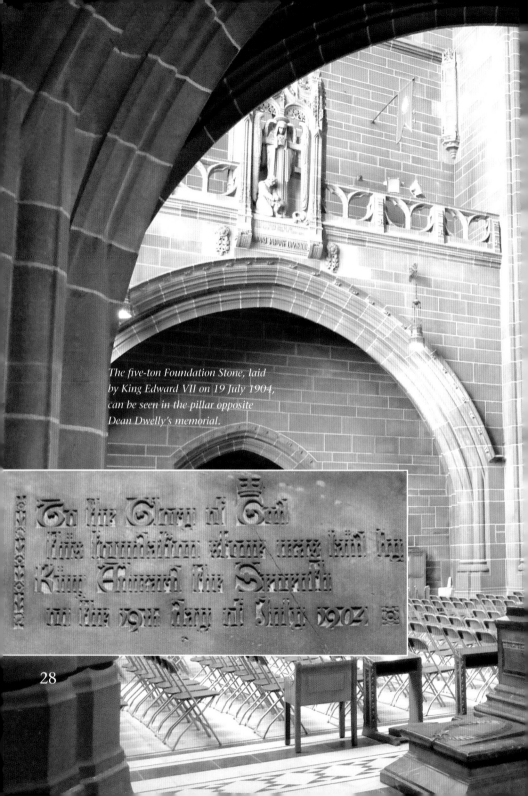

The five-ton Foundation Stone, laid by King Edward VII on 19 July 1904, can be seen in the pillar opposite Dean Dwelly's memorial.

Whispering Arch ∞

The arch in the east transept demonstrate an acoustic quirk: a person whispering into the stone on one side of the arch can be heard clearly by someone on the other side.

The bronze memorial is to the 16th Earl of Derby who died in 1908, a generous benefactor to the Cathedral and first chairman of the Cathedral Committee.

God in the small things

Britain's ancient cathedrals used art and crafts to illustrate and proclaim the Christian message. Scott's 20th century masterpiece is no different. Stone angels look down from the lofty perches in all parts of the building, and a multitude of God's creatures can be found in ironwork, glass and woodcarvings. Flowers of the field abound.

Perhaps the most popular of these animals is to be found on the memorial to the Earl of Derby in the east transept. A mouse peeps shyly from behind the cushion close to the Earl's head. Visitors also enjoy the pairs of Liverbirds – symbols of Liverpool – which guard the steps to the choir stalls.

The snail and the salamander in the ironwork of the 'Alleluia Door' on the north side of the Lady Chapel are not to be missed.

Liverpool Cathedral

Animal
Safari
Activity Book

Join Derby Mouse and his friends in the Cathedral for puzzles, quizzes and fun!

30

31

David Sheppard Memorial

Unveiled in 2011, an arresting memorial commemorates the extraordinary ministry of David Sheppard, Bishop of Liverpool from 1975 to 1997. The iconic partnership between Bishop Sheppard and Archbishop Derek Warlock of the Roman Catholic Archdiocese of Liverpool transformed ecumenical relationships in a city with a history of sectarian division.

A statue to both men now stands, fittingly, half way down Hope Sreet (at either end of which stand Liverpool's two cathedrals).

A white Portland stone is set in a carved recess of the sandstone wall of the Cathedral. The smooth surface of the white stone is not flawless, for only God is without blemish. The white stone is set at a height where visitors are able to touch it.

Beneath a plaque in the floor, below the memorial, the ashes of both Bishop David and his wife Grace are interred.

A biblical text loops around the memorial, taken from Jeremiah 29.7: 'Seek the welfare of the city where I have sent you…and pray to the Lord on its behalf'.

33

The Font

The font stands in the south west transept, known as the Baptistery. The importance of baptism to the Christian community is emphasised by the almost 40-foot high (12m) oak baldachino (ornamental canopy). The font cover, 15 feet high (4.6m), also of oak, rests lightly on the marble font itself and is ingeniously counter-balanced by a 17cwt stone in the cover itself so that it can rise and fall easily.

Jesus was baptised at the start of his public ministry, and commanded his followers to baptise new disciples. This has been the constant practice of the church for 2000 years.

The floor surround is made of marble, inlaid with swirling, breaking waves and a circle of green fishes – the fish being an ancient symbol of Christianity.

© Liverpool Cathedral

The font is made of unusual buff-coloured French marble and has the figure of an apostle carved in relief by E. Carter Preston on each of its 12 sides.

Elizabeth Hoare (a niece of Sir Giles Gilbert Scott), ran Watts and Company — a famous ecclesiastical embroiderers in London which had been founded by G. F. Bodley. She was thus well-placed to collect discarded altar frontals and vestments and over the years she became an authority on ecclesiastical needlework.

Her private collection of embroidery was outstanding and in 1992 she presented it to the Cathedral. It is now on display in a gallery at triforium level where it can be seen by visitors on the way to the top of the tower.

The Pre-Raphaelite style is characteristic of many of the drawings and embroideries in the Hoare Collection.

Agnus·Dei·dona·nobis·pacem

The
Embroideries
at Liverpool Cathedral

tem tuam

This guide is available in the Cathedral Shop

Sunset from the Tower

FACT FILE

The tower is 100m (331 feet) tall making a spectacular landmark and view point.

The tower is named after the Vestey family who contributed the money for its construction.

The Vestey family gave over £300,000 for the building of the tower and a memorial to Baron Vestey can be seen beneath it in the Central Space.

The top of the tower can be reached by two separate lifts and 108 steps.

Photo © Liverpool Cathedral